TEN COMMANDMENTS OF
FINANCIAL FREEDOM

TEN COMMANDMENTS
OF FINANCIAL FREEDOM

Luis Estrada

ISBN: 153323292X
ISBN 13: 9781533232922
Library of Congress Control Number: 2016908121
CreateSpace Independent Publishing Platform
North Charleston, South Carolina

Note

This book should not be taken as a specific solution or particular financial advice. Readers must research and seek professional financial advice based on their particular objectives, incomes, ages, and family and retirement plans, as well as tax and estate planning.

Contents

Note ·v

Preface · ix

Chapter 1   You shall save. · 1

Chapter 2   You shall be wary of almost any form
of debt.· 5

Chapter 3   You shall be wary of systems that promise
to make you rich soon.· 8

Chapter 4   You shall remember in good times that
there will come times of scarcity and crisis. · · · · · · · · 10

Chapter 5   You shall not overinvest; always have
some cash reserved. · 14

Chapter 6   You shall know that the stock market
is for the long term and requires discipline
and study.· 16

Chapter 7   You shall sell when everybody buys and
buy when everybody sells. · 20

Chapter 8   You shall invest in assets that generate
             cash/income.· 22
Chapter 9   You shall use compounding. · 24
Chapter 10   You shall diversify—moderately. · · · · · · · · · · · · · · · · · 26

             Emotions· 31
             The Economy in the Future · 33

Preface

I wake up fearful of a financial Armageddon. This is curious because the financial investments are minimal, and the prospects of adding more are reduced. Once a true believer in the financial markets, I have come to realize how the lack of ethics has adversely played out in the world of finances.

The problem with the lack of ethics is that the rules of the game are constructed unfairly, manipulated, or unobserved outright due to the complacency of those supposedly charged with the task of oversight and surveillance. It is astounding how a fund may lose track of billions of investors' money without much consequence other than the investors' savings being erased from the face of the earth. It is astounding how a single employee has the ability to operate and risk billions of dollars as though playing roulette in Las Vegas.

Governments have also lost serenity, composure, reason, and ethics. How is it possible that a government assumes a great deal of public debt—that is, a debt that at some point must be paid by citizens who played no role in deciding to indebt their country?

Another rotten element is many financial media outlets. They also contribute to this culture defined by a lack of ethics. They provide information that is superficial, with an expiration date of a couple of hours, ready to be disposed of by the readers as a result of the lack of depth. For the most part, it is all about hidden interests behind an article, an interview, or a column.

Within this context, one must ask which, if any, vehicles exist for the preservation and growth of the money one has worked so hard to earn. Now, consider that the money by itself will lose value as governments debase their currencies by printing more money. I remember a basic example from my economics class. If there are three apples and three dollars, each apple costs one dollar. But if we print three additional dollars, apples will then cost two dollars each. The price of each apple increases as a result of more dollars being available. That is how our savings in the form of money lose value over time.

Since governments have become these enormous borrowing and spending beasts, the need for money increases substantially; hence, governments put the presses to work and borrow issuing notes. You are the ultimate payer of these by way of taxation and lower-quality public services.

Make no mistake: that is a chief idea in the world of managing wealth. And I believe the first mistake you must avoid is allowing other people to manage your money. Why would you trust someone to take care of your money if managing it is even easier than making it? Do you really think that an investment specialist, investment expert, or investment advisor—call it whatever you like—will put as much care as you would in preserving and growing what is yours?

Financial institutions and advisors have made enough money for themselves for people to lose any trust and confidence in them. I am not an insider. I do not need to be one to realize the degree of decay in the financial world that brought us to the 2007–2008 subprime mortgage crisis.

Now, there is good news. Managing one's own money is not as difficult as it may appear. You do not need to be a businessperson, but you must get your own education about how to manage your own money. Do not be a financial dwarf. I have summarized ten main rules to follow that simplify and lay out the basis for managing and growing wealth. I call them the ten commandments of financial independence.

1. You shall save.
2. You shall be wary of any form of debt.
3. You shall be wary of systems that promise to make you rich soon.
4. You shall remember in good times that there will come times of scarcity and crisis.
5. You shall not overinvest; always have some cash reserved.
6. You shall know that the stock market is for the long term and requires discipline and study.
7. You shall sell when everybody buys and buy when everybody sells.

8. You shall invest in assets that produce cash/income.
9. You shall use compounding.
10. You shall diversify—moderately.

Following these rules will have an enormous positive effect in your life. I have put them in a way that is easy to understand and to follow.

1

You shall save.

One has to find a personal motivation for saving. I remember an elderly person who once told me that his motivation for saving was that he did not want to die poor. He had been a poor country boy, he had suffered from hunger and thirst, and he was afraid to become old and poor. He decided to become financially independent and create wealth, and he achieved his dream out of fear in order to avoid the misery he had experienced in the early stages of his life.

He did it. He made a considerable amount of money out of his business and by saving. Still, he measured the number of water gallons he used at home, halved his cigarettes, and avoided expensive luxuries. He only changed cars on four or five occasions in his life.

Saving requires having an income and spending less than we take in. The difference is the amount that we can save. But remember that we must pay taxes. Some people get in trouble because they forget that taxes come first. Taxes are our contribution to society for all the public services that we get from the government, such as schools, roads, police, judges, and so on. Therefore, it is an important duty to pay taxes on our incomes. A good accountant or tax advisor should help us minimize the amount of taxes we pay, as the law always has some benefits or allowances that apply under certain conditions. For example, when you have kids, tax laws allow you to deduct a certain amount for each child that is free of taxes.

Spending less than you take in requires discipline, determination, and a good deal of will. We will have to give up some things that we like or that we think we need. Saving requires self-control, and to tell you the truth, it is a central part of building wealth. Saving is deferred compensation: enjoy later but enjoy more.

Some people spend without control. They spend as a way to fill the voids in their lives, but the more they spend, the greater the void. Spending is not a way to find comfort or validation. It usually leads to financial ruin.

Keep track of your expenses. Having a budget and keeping track of your expenses are both helpful in identifying saving opportunities. But do not restrain yourself to only one formula. Each individual is different, and there may be as many methods of controlling expenses as there are people. I will give you an example. For some time, my saving method consisted of putting money away in a bank account after I paid taxes and took care of all my day-to-day expenses. However, I often took money from my bank account when I succumbed to the temptation to spend. A solution I found was to buy real estate, which I paid in installments with financing from the developer. That way, I knew I could not spend money because I had to pay each installment. Of course, that form of saving had one inconvenience in that I had to pay interest, and the net amount saved was less than what I could have saved had I not paid interest. Nonetheless, the method was good for me, as I avoided a more expensive choice: taking it all from the bank account to buy nonessential stuff.

Saving also implies using things carefully and maintaining them in good shape in order to extend their useful lives. It implies avoiding buying new models if our gadgets are still able to provide us with reasonable service.

On one occasion, I felt frustrated because I could not persuade my thirteen-year-old son to make the correct financial decision about a last-minute purchase of a jersey and a pair of golf shoes. We first went to a high-end sports store, where a pair of golf shoes cost $220, but it carried no golf shirts. I thanked the salesperson, and we headed to a second-tier sports store. They had a golf shirt for $150 but carried no golf shoes. (At this point, my son had fallen in love with the shoes in the first store and the shirt in the second one). I set off for a third store to continue the hunt, when my son said, "Dad, we are set; we found them. We can buy the shoes at the first store and the shirt at the second. Where are we going?" I replied that we were going to a third store to check prices and quality. When we got to the third store, the least promising of the three, I found what I considered the ideal deal: a pair of golf shoes from a competing brand for one hundred dollars and a golf shirt of an unrecognized brand (but that looked nicer and felt better knitted and more resistant) for about forty-seven dollars. But that was not the whole deal. This store would give us a thirty-dollar gift certificate for the purchase of the golf shoes, which would bring the total cost of both the shoes and the shirt to $117.

My preppy child did not like the shirt and decided to take the one for $150 that he had tried on at the second store plus the one-hundred-dollar shoes, bringing the total cost of our golf tour to $250. From there, my litany about how to spend wisely and save money became a real threat to our golfing the next day.

Saving is not an option; it is a must. Saving requires refraining from impulses. It helps build confidence and self-control. It is an important part of the virtue of prudence that enables us to foresee those means necessary to achieve our goals.

You shall be wary of almost any form of debt.

D ebt is not a good friend to financial independence and growth— especially credit-card debt. One way I like to describe debt is like a huge black beast with large claws and edgy teeth tied by a chain to a pole. If you keep away from the pole, the beast can't harm you. But if you decide to get close to the beast, it will tear you apart.

Many people who once had considerable wealth have seen their financial failure as a result of incurring debt. Debt is bad because of the interest we pay. The cost of borrowing money is called interest. If you want to rent a car for one day, the company will charge you a certain amount of money. It is the same with money: if you want to borrow money for a certain period of time, you will have to return the money loaned to you (principal) plus more money for having used it (interest). This makes it expensive.

Borrowing money is not wise, especially when the things you buy with the borrowed money do not produce cash or, if they produce it, do so at a lesser rate than the interest you pay for the borrowed money. Do not borrow money. It is better to loan money than to borrow it because then your money will start working for you.

If you want to be smart about managing money, use it in a way that you do not lose it. Spending is a way of losing your money because you will never see that money again. It is gone forever. Moreover, the things that you buy may require more spending in order to maintain or use them.

Mr. Carlos Slim's father used to teach his children that money that leaves the company will never return. Carlos Slim is now one of the richest people in the world. He owns telephone companies, banks, stores, insurance companies, and mining and infrastructure companies. Companies with no debt or minimum levels of debt are successful, and potential investors like you should prefer them over other types of companies.

In addition to the fact that borrowing money costs us more money, one of the main problems with borrowing money is that we cannot anticipate that the same conditions that exist at the time when we borrow will continue during the life of the loan. We may see our incomes decline or lose our jobs, our businesses may face sudden changes including dropping sales, the economy may turn downward, and so on. If you are tied to a loan, you will have to pay regardless of what is going on in your life, with your business, or with the economy. If this was true for our parents and grandparents, it is more so for us since changes come so much faster now in the labor force, the economy, global commerce, and international finance.

And how about leverage (acquiring assets with a small investment supplemented with borrowed money)? This could work as long as the investment is already generating the necessary income to pay the borrowed money.

There are instances where debt is good and makes sense. But we are dealing with the basics. Eventually, you will learn how to handle and manage debt wisely to your own advantage. In the meantime, do not get close to the beast. Keep away!

3

You shall be wary of systems that
promise to make you rich soon.

Unfortunately, becoming financially independent fast is not usually the way it works. It takes working hard, learning, saving, and putting your money to work. It is not easy, but it is relatively easier than we imagine. The problem is that we are not taught the basic facts of wealth creation and financial independence. Most of the time, we have to learn after having made many mistakes. We all make mistakes on our way to wealth creation, but the sooner we learn, the better.

One mistake we must avoid is investing in anything that promises us that we are going to become wealthy with the swing of a magic wand. Many of those methods are basically schemes to profit off desperate and naïve people. Avoid them. If you work for yourself or someone else, pay your taxes, save, put your money to work, reinvest, and be patient, you will create wealth and be financially independent.

These traps and fraudulent schemes take on a variety of forms. Do not fall into the hands of unscrupulous people. If you think it is too good to be true, it probably is. What should you do in these cases? Ask the opinions of people who are well informed. Do your research. Question yourself. These types of schemes are sometimes very sophisticated.

4

You shall remember in good times
that there will come times of
scarcity and crisis.

Keeping this in mind is always important and is the foundation of savings. As we discussed, savings is an essential element of building wealth. Savings may take two basic forms: liquid and nonliquid assets. Both are important. Liquid assets, also called cash, give us the ability to be solvent in our financial obligations when the economy and our businesses face difficult times. They also afford us the great chance of acquiring assets at a much lower price when other people need to sell them to obtain much-needed cash. Acquiring assets at a discount or below market value is a manner of building wealth, especially if they can be turned into investments that produce income rapidly, such as rental income, dividends, and interests. The trick to financial gain is not selling expensive (as any market pretty much sets that price for us), but buying at a low price. The gain is in the latter.

Be prepared. When you hire people or make capital investments, think of the way you can most effectively get rid of those without losing money in the event that the economy turns sour.

Be patient. With social media and the Internet, there may be a perception that everyone has to be rich at a young age. Though this may be true for some, the vast majority of us must look to the long run. If we think that way, then time works in our favor rather than against us. Of course, that is only true if we are patient and avoid the mistakes that many people make in their hurry to get rich.

Time makes it easier, not more difficult. You have more experience, and you have more assets as your savings have increased, which means you have more money to put to work. You have learned from mistakes, and you have acquired knowledge.

Impatience brings errors and hurried decisions without proper pondering and consideration. Want to increase your wealth? Be patient. Be analytical. Observe. Don't worry about the pace or speed of others. You are your own person. Do not try to catch up with anybody.

If you compare yourself to others or try to live in an expensive way beyond your means, you will lose it all. I remember a real-estate and escrow agent who became too ambitious during the best time for the real-estate market. With a lot of money coming in, she became too ambitious. It seemed that she was not getting enough. She wanted to go faster, so faster she went—straight down. She took the money she had in escrow and put it in the stock market. The market came crashing down, and so did she and the people who had entrusted closings to her. She is out of business and has ruined her reputation, and she became a fugitive of the law.

Another good measure of prudence is to beware of luxury living among those who manage money for others. I remember assisting a friend in recovering some of the money he had lost to a financial advisor who lacked any ethics, conscience, and professional honor. During one of the talks we had, I asked my friend if he had ever noticed anything strange or abnormal when dealing with his advisor. His response was that he'd noticed the expensive cars the advisor drove and the expensive clothing and watches he always wore.

Do not make any assumptions. Do not follow the crowd. As a matter of fact, most of the time, you will do better by not following the crowd. Go in the other direction.

I had an uncle who loved homing pigeons. He owned many, raised them, observed them, and traded them. It was his passion and hobby. He was also as successful a businessman as you could find. He would take the pigeons many miles out and release them to find their way back home. But after some years of experience, when he wanted to identify which ones had conditions successful for breeding, he started to release them one by one on a single basis.

One of his sons asked why he had changed to a single release instead of releasing them together. His answer was extraordinarily good for the purposes of the point I want to make here. If you release them one by one, you immediately notice if each one went the right direction right away. If you release them altogether, the flock will follow the first pigeon with initiative. The same happens in dealing with financial matters. In following the flock, you might be following people that are going the wrong direction as a result of following a mistaken (or misleading) leader. Be your own leader, know your destination, and go there, making adjustments when necessary.

5

You shall not overinvest; always have some cash reserved.

This commandment goes hand in hand with number four. Cash or liquid assets are essential to make agile, rapid turns or adjustments when difficulty comes or a great opportunity presents itself. When you have all of your resources invested in nonliquid assets, the ability to modify your strategy in a short time is diminished. Even if your business income or the salary you earn is good, and you want to put it all to work for you, you need to know that some adversities will come about sooner or later. If you have it all invested, forget it. You will be forced to sell at very low prices.

I once met a person who had a bed-and-breakfast in a beach tourist destination. The business was thriving. He had a good cash flow, so he decided to invest it all and assume some debt to start another B&B at the same destination. He bought a used property and renovated it, but the business never worked. He lost out greatly.

Sometimes it is better to buy a business that is already going and has the client base and income instead of starting from the beginning. Many people who have been forced to sell under disadvantageous conditions were overinvested or did not have a clear idea of the income expectations that would be needed for the new investment. Cash is always necessary. Do not use it or invest it all.

Some people may find it difficult to have cash because they feel tempted to use or spend it. One solution may be to have it invested in thirty- or sixty-day CDs that reinvest it automatically. That way you know that the money cannot be touched.

6

You shall know that the stock market
is for the long term and requires
discipline and study.

As with everything in life, long-term thinking and discipline are important. Rapid gratification is not found in investing. Following the performance of the companies you hold and the trends dominating the environment where these companies work is important. That is why it is better to have only a few holdings so that tracking them is feasible. You do not need shares in a large number of companies.

Many specialists, advisors, and brokers will recommend the funds with which they are familiar. This makes sense prima facie. But how do you know that what they are familiar with is a good investment? That is why there is no substitute for learning about, being informed about, reading about, and being familiar with as much information as possible relating to the companies you invest in. A number of aids and tools exist, such as magazines, periodicals, TV financial channels, analyses from banks and brokerage firms, SEC filings, and company releases. After a while, you will become quite knowledgeable and able to make your own decisions about your own money. You may even give a tip or two to a broker.

Ask as many questions as possible, and never be shy about inquiring on issues that you may not know about or understand. Nobody can manage your portfolio as you can—nobody.

Do not get into investing instruments that you have not studied and do not understand. The concept of owning shares in a company is not too complicated. But getting into derivatives, such as options and swaps, is another thing. Do not play with fire. Investing should not be about adrenaline or excitement. If you are looking for that, go to Las Vegas. This is about protecting and increasing your hard-earned money and the rest of your assets.

Following the investment moves and opinions of recognized active investors and fund managers with recognized success records is another way to improve your portfolio. But always make sure you understand the reasons for your decisions and feel comfortable with them.

I continuously hear investment specialists say that it is too difficult for common individuals to track companies and their shares, and for that reason, the obvious recommendation is to invest in those funds that their companies market. They almost unanimously stress the advantage of their companies operating various funds with different risk levels suited for different client profiles. You are your own client. Another option is to invest in market indexes. These follow the performance of the market as a whole, and you do not have to keep track of specific companies if you lack the time or the ability to do so.

You will hear many arguments that the compensation of fund managers is tied to fund performance and that, therefore, you should trust that the fund manager will try hard to make your money profit. In many instances this could be true. However, investing in index-tied funds has a great advantage: avoiding institutions that have aggressively pushed greatly dangerous or risky instruments down the throats of their customers. Why wait ten years to guess which kind of institution or manager you have in charge of your hard-earned money?

I seriously believe that we should not give up the responsibility of managing our own money. Invest in what you like and what you have researched to be a sound company. Simple stock investment is one of the great concepts of capitalism. Imagine that you are sitting in a plane, and the person next to you asks, "What do you do for a living?" You say you are a lawyer, teacher, or whatever you do. Then you add, "I am also one of the owners of Coca-Cola." That would certainly impress anyone. But that would also be totally true if you own stock in Coca-Cola, IBM, or any other great company. And that is what the stock market offers people: to share or participate in owning a piece of a given company.

Would you invest in any company? Of course not. You need to profile which type of company will make your investment grow. That is where you need to do your work—work that may be fascinating since it will introduce you to numbers and facts. No other investing argument will be as powerful and accurate as the numbers and facts behind a company.

You do not have to like or use a product that a specific company manufactures or markets. What you do need to like is the money that the company makes, its potential for growth, and the efficiency with which the management operates that business. This is another advantage of capitalism. What would it take for you or me to get a great management team together and the resources needed to run a company?

Which factors should you consider when examining a particular company? Warren Buffet has said that past performance with continuous years of profit generation, low levels of debt, and great management teams are the most important aspects. He would go for stand-alone products rather than more complex operations.

You and I certainly do not have the time and expertise that Warren Buffet or other active, extremely successful investors have. But we do have the ability to understand basic concepts such as debt, book value, number or shares, return, dividends paid, earnings, and so on. Moreover, if this task becomes a burden, we can still follow the recommendations and moves of the great American investors.

7

You shall sell when everybody buys
—and buy when everybody sells.

I s this easy to say and difficult to do? Yes. This basic and true investing principle seems more obvious than the sun coming up every morning. Yet the fear of holding on to a stock when its price is declining is so great that emotion overrides reason. If you bought prime quality, then hold on to it. Additionally, since you are following commandment five, your cash will allow you to buy a little bit more of it. When the price is up, you may want to sell a small portion. Dividend-paying stocks should be your favorite since the cash they generate will accelerate your growth.

Remember that you are building for the long run. When investing, do not use money that you definitely need for other short-term necessities because that would lead you to sell at the wrong time. Do not think that there is only one opportunity. Be patient. Your patience will be rewarded. If you feel the temptation to buy more than you need, distract yourself by researching companies that may fit into the model you have designed and that have been hiding from you. Take a walk, or smoke a cigarette—maybe a brand whose stock you own—but refrain from that destructive impulse.

Look at the list of billionaires. You will find more than one who made a great chunk of that wealth in the stock market through discipline and patience. You will not become rich from one day to the next, but you certainly will over the decades. If you feel the impulse to buy more when you already know that you are sufficiently invested, that means that you are not reading enough. You have too much time free that you might use to increase the flow from your usual work, employment, or business.

If you do not have enough cash reserved, you will miss those opportunities that may present themselves only once or twice in your lifetime when you can buy at incredibly low prices. You will not only need the money to buy those cheap stocks, but you will also need it to survive because, in those exceptionally good times to buy stocks, your otherwise normal lead source of income will most probably be seriously challenged.

But how do you know which level to sell and buy at? Don't worry; nobody knows for sure. You will make many mistakes in terms of having missed highs or lows. But rather than jumping on and off, try to focus on maintaining and preserving those exceptionally good companies that will give you growth over the years. You will develop a relative sense of where the shares you own are sailing to.

8

You shall invest in assets that generate cash/income.

When investing, you may want to consider stocks that generate income most basically through dividends. Look where we are; we are at commandment eight, not one or two. While income generation is important, do not miss the most important issues of all when buying stocks: the history of the company and the verifiable history of revenue, cash flow, and growth. Be wary of inconsistencies along the way. Be skeptical of new companies. You may make tons of money, but you may lose it as well. If the company passes your test, a plus is the payment of dividends to a level that does not impair its ability to grow and reinvest. One thing for sure is that the company that does not reinvest in its own business has its days counted.

Investing in assets that generate income seems a very obvious and self-evident principle. Yet many people, even wealthy ones, fail to observe it, at least in stages where one would think that more cash or wealth must be built before jumping into the specu-lation phase. Whether that is because of impulsive behavior or any other reason, it is important to stress that we must favor income generation. A cow that is fed but produces no milk is not a good investment.

9

You shall use compounding.

This is the eighth wonder of the world. The same interest that may send you off the cliff when you do not pay the total of your credit-card balance may make you rich when you reinvest all interest and dividends over your lifetime. This is marvelous. A multiplying effect is the steroids of finance.

The intent of generating income is not so that you get a check out of your account every once in a while. It is for you to reinvest all incoming cash so that you enjoy the benefits of compounding, a great ally of any good investor. It is an accelerator that, over the years, will give you good compensation. It is money producing money and reinvesting it so that those earnings produce more money. Do not waste time. Want to reach millionaire status? Understand and apply the concept of compounding. It is the baking powder in any good investment kitchen.

Think of compounding as a snowball. It increases the value of your money, creating a higher mass at a faster pace.

10

You shall diversify—moderately.

Last but not least is the need for moderate diversification. Warren Buffet once said that diversification is protection against ignorance. You do not want to put all your eggs in the same basket. However, this diversification needs to be moderate so that you can keep a record, follow those companies, and make any necessary adjustments. How many? You will know.

The stock market is a serious form of investment that requires many virtues. Never get too proud about good results, but never get too sad when downturns occur. Every investor will have bad years. But every year is only a battle in a multi-decade war. Expect to make the most errors in the first years, but you will learn and develop expertise and knowledge. Investing is not gambling. Do not trust your gut or others' guts. Rely only on facts and verified information.

How much time can you devote daily to analyzing numbers, following news, reading charts, comparing SEC filings, immersing yourself into balance sheets, and trying to detect accounting makeups? One hour? A half? Fifteen minutes? It is worth doing it!

Organize yourself better, and you will find the time. To this work, you can add the input of research companies.

You live in America. You should never be afraid of investing for and by yourself. The cost structure of mutual funds, traders' commissions, or periods of highly unethical behavior in the industry may justify taking control of your own finances. But there is still one deeper and more compelling reason: no one will do the same job as you of caring and growing your own wealth. This is not rhetoric. This is a simple, basic fact. Do it hands on!

At this point, we should discuss a few of the many arguments against investing in stocks. The market is manipulated through a variety of cheating practices, including insider trading, high-frequency trading, conflicts of interest with active advisors who push stocks or other instruments for the primary benefit of their brokerage firms, claims that the system is rigged, and so on. Yes, indeed, these and many other unfair, though not always unlawful, practices work against the individual investor. Yet investing in well-established companies with proven dividend records or in funds following a particular index over the long run can be a good strategy. Avoiding buying and selling and reaching for the short-run gain will get you out of the expensive commissions that brokers charge no matter what the fee system. All of the existing trading platforms are another way to save in commissions.

In the end, we should encourage ourselves not to trade but to invest. Remember that we are not looking for adrenaline and excitement or killing time by seeing what good guessers we are.

Beating the market for a few months or years is not the main purpose. The purpose is to invest in companies. You are buying a share of a company's assets and liabilities, cash flow, experience, dividend payment record, market share, position, good will, growth capacity, and so on.

You may have heard this argument time and again, but buy when it is cheap and keep, sustain, maintain, watch, observe, and ask. Picturing a comparison to a nonpublic company may help. Which questions would you ask a neighbor who comes into your home, inviting you to invest in the great company that he or she owns? List ten questions you would ask in that hypothetical situation.

1._____   6. _____

2._____   7. _____

3._____   8. _____

4._____   9. _____

5._____   10._____

Remember that the idea is not to discover the next big Apple or Google. These types of companies may go one way or another. You do not want to guess whether an idea will work or will have a market for it. You want to be with a company that has been around for many years with many shareholders, great cash flow, and a low level of debt, leading market position, and dividend rates attractive to your expectations and not too high to impede reinvestment.

In the end, you are beating the ever-decreasing value of fiat money and being covered under the wings of an entity that produces wealth. Over time, it should work. Any company may fail or go bad. But there is always the possibility for a company to thrive even in hard times and economic downturns. Look for these.

Emotions

An important factor to consider is the emotional side of investing. Unfortunately, many investing strategies fail because of emotional interference. Investing is an activity that requires analysis and rational thinking—a cold approach to facts. Instead, many people are tempted to make decisions based on adrenaline or fantasy and imagination. Irrational behavior assumes control, and the results are negative. How to keep our emotions in line is a task for each of us to discover. Investing is not a gambling activity where leisure and luck play a core role. In gambling, we are part players and part witnesses with results left to chance. It does not matter that we participate; we are, for the most part, witnesses with little control over the results. Data is disorganized and not analyzed.

Instead, investing should be the result of thinking, comparing, analyzing, and examining data and background information. Filter, question, judge, and doubt all the information and recommendations coming your way.

If you take care of your family, health, and business, there is no reason for you not to take care of your personal finances yourself. Do not be lazy. You must assume that you have the potential and inner ability to make yourself financially independent.

Keep your wits sharp, your guts tight, and your intake of daily financial information constant. Save and invest. Do not depend on others. You do not depend on the government but on your job. You can make money and put it to work. Start now. Do not procrastinate. Do it.

The Economy in the Future

Economies of different countries always have good and bad times. Ages of prosperity follow ages of scarcity and poverty. The fascinating thing is that in both good and bad times, there will always be companies that will thrive because of good management, good service, a dominant position, reasonable leverage, and reinvesting.

Whether the economy is good or bad should not matter much as long as each cycle gets us prepared with cash, without debt, and with a positive mind-set. When the economy gets sour, the ones who suffer first are those swimming in debt. Avoid paying interest. Do not buy what you cannot afford. Whether it is social peer or another type of induced pressure, ignore it. Do not crave things you do not need and do not have the money to pay for in cash. Yes, cash. Forgot about cash? Not carrying a balance on your credit cards is the most financially sound decision you will ever make. If you are credit mad, it is time to fix the house and reduce your balance to zero. You may have to get some help in order to quit buying those things that you do not need.

But what can we expect next from the world economy? First, we have to understand that the economy has changed forever, and it will never be the same. Remember having a job, paying your bills, getting a mortgage and a loan for your car, and retiring after years of saving? No more. Governments all around the world are, for the most part, making the creation of jobs a more and more difficult venture. Creating jobs is much more difficult for companies than it has ever been. There are myriad reasons. Some countries impose huge employment taxes and welfare charges; others affect job creation indirectly by impeding competition as they seek to maintain the status quo of their political and economic elites. Others use unions to feed their never-ending hunger for political power, to the detriment of job creation. While the amount of wealth and output is the same, it must be shared by companies and the government. But more and more, the world is deciding to send a bigger piece of the pie to the governments. At the same time, governments debase their currencies and try to create inflation. This creates a double-down effect on the negative impacts of wealth creation.

What does this affect in our lives, beyond the inherent negative impact on our liberties and freedom? It gets harder for the common person to earn enough and save for retirement. In the end, the answer lies in each of us designing our financial independence.

Will this ever change? I do not foresee it in the near future. Governments are now insatiable bureaucracies that are encroaching on people's lives in an unprecedented way. The cost of running governments and their policies is rising, and consequently, public debt is too. Take inflation, for example. Isn't it ridiculous that the costs of our basic needs go up relentlessly at a higher pace and speed than those that the inflation-rate indexes show? I like to picture this as a race between one person—who wants to make it to the end and save—and a turbocharged racing car. The latter is inflation. Any government would suck value from currency if given the chance, and they do have that chance. What that means is that your hard-earned money will lose value faster. Therefore, the answer is to find the best allocation of resources at hand to multiply the value of our money. Generate enough flow to make the flow even larger and larger. This is hard. But don't be confused. With time, it gets easier.

Income depression is affecting the economy as people spend less and fall behind the cost of living. Also, the skills people have are becoming rapidly outdated. We are in a new century and a new millennium. Changes are happening too fast and will continue to happen that way. The skills necessary to do a job are not good enough when the need for that job no longer exists. Therefore, we must optimize our incomes and avoid any debt and expenses that may derail that income from its full potential. Job security is lower than ever, and that pattern will be the new state of things in the labor market.

Wage stagnation affecting the middle and lower classes is really a threat to safety all around the globe. Instead of alleviating the situation by lowering taxes and easing overregulation for job creators, governments try to compensate for this with welfare unemployment and food benefits, creating a social distortion. We must consider if an economy based on credit is desirable or if we need to change to another model, especially when we seem to be on the verge of very difficult times ahead.

All of the accommodative policies that the Fed put in place after the 2008 financial crisis, including the mass public debt created thereafter, were not matched with lower taxes, deregulation, and significant public-spending reduction. For decades, the IMF and the World Bank have preached to emerging economies that in order to achieve acceptable GDP growth rates, they should reduce public debt and nonproductive public spending, increase exports, and encourage internal savings. Now it seems that, for whatever reason, the United States is doing exactly what other countries have repeatedly been told not to do over the decades.

Another outdated institution is the measurement of GDP. It seems a game played over and over for central banks and other institutions to forecast a rate of GDP growth, only to later adjust their outlook downward. Some countries have gone to the extreme of including prostitution and drug-related activities as a way to be able to show less dismaying figures. This is a clear indication that the current situation is not sustainable. Again, government intervention is the main cause of this environment.

More and more people should be encouraged to be self-employed or become entrepreneurs and leave behind the dependence where one day you have a job and the next you are downsized. This is a hazard as well as an opportunity.

While governments continue to encroach in people's lives, the cost of doing business will increase. This will have a negative effect on small businesses all over the world. And let us please not forget that small businesses account for more job creation than any other type of business.

Now, job security will no longer be the case. But becoming self-employed or an entrepreneur will be more difficult as the burden of regulatory and governmental oversight increases. Only major companies will be able to afford such regulatory burdens. The alternative is to create a company in those fields that are not overregulated and that add value for its customers in ways that secure their survival. Or you can invest in a public company and forget about the hassle.

Believe it or not, skilled work where both physical and mental abilities are required will do increasingly well. This includes electricians, drivers, plumbers, and carpenters. On the contrary, certain professional jobs will be less in demand. In times of crises and economic hardship, intangibles are more difficult to sell.

There is other factor that will hold the economy down. The population growth rate around the globe is pretty low. If you think about it, kids generate the bulk of expenditure in any economy: tuition, clothing, doctors, food, vaccines, medicine, amusement, books, and so on. There is no spending like that needed to raise a family, yet the Malthusian thinking has percolated throughout public policies and individual thought all over. The number of homes available due to baby boomers moving to smaller spaces or retirement communities is very high. I have visited these homes in various cities, and I do not think that there are enough families to absorb these inventories of existing homes while at the same time having a dynamic new-home-construction industry—not unless new families are formed and these families decide to have children. But again this raises the question of how they will do it if wages are poor. It is a vicious circle now created by government policies. Young people cannot find jobs, and they decide to postpone getting married and having kids, two social behaviors that historically help the economy. Kids are the engine of the economy since they drive consumption across the broad fiscal spectrum.

Another big problem is the increasing regulation for starting up businesses. Although this red tape affects all groups, it has a negative impact on young people who want to become self-employed as a result of job scarcity. This is accompanied by yet another distortion created by governments: social welfare. If the benefits of welfare are too generous in terms of money or time length, incentives to look for a job or become self-employed are removed.

Wealth concentration is another reason to be concerned about our economic future. Perhaps, as a kid, you got to play a board game called Monopoly. This game seemed very interesting to me. It could teach you many interesting facts about the real-world economy and personal finance. But the most important lesson for me was a pattern that I observed every time I played the game with my siblings or friends: when one or two players accumulated the majority of properties and cash, the pace of the activity really decreased to almost a total stall. I believe that this same effect is replicated in real-world economies. Specifically damaging is the hit that the middle class is taking. There is nothing wrong with creating billionaires. On the contrary, I have nothing against it. Nonetheless, the stress inflicted on the middle class is of great concern both socially and economically. The middle class is highly vulnerable as it is the most extensive component of the social fabric. To help the members of the middle class, governments must do the following:

- Lower taxes for job creators.
- Reduce public spending.
- Increase tax allowances for each kid.
- Control welfare benefits (unemployment and food).
- Deregulate all nonfinancial activities.
- Impose harder penalties and sanctions on finance-related activities.
- Reduce public deficit.

For assets to increase their values, consumption is necessary, and consumption requires population growth, good wages, and few barriers to investment.

For many individuals, the time has come to take financial matters into their own hands. Good luck, and remember that it takes time, discipline, prudence, courage, and patience. But you can do it!